To Soph—P.C.

To Michael Lawrence, who bridges the gaps—R.D.

SIMON & SCHUSTER BOOKS FOR YOUNG READERS
Simon & Schuster Building, Rockefeller Center, 1230 Avenue of the
Americas, New York, New York 10020. Text copyright © 1992 by Polly *Copy 2*
Carter. Illustrations copyright © 1992 by Roy Doty. All rights reserved
including the right of reproduction in whole or in part in any form.
SIMON & SCHUSTER BOOKS FOR YOUNG READERS
is a trademark of Simon & Schuster.
The text of this book is set in Goudy.
The illustrations were done in pen and ink.
Manufactured in the United States of America

10   9   8   7   6   5   4   3   2   1

Library of Congress Cataloging-in-Publication Data
Carter, Polly. The bridge book / by Polly Carter; illustrated by Roy Doty.
p. cm. Summary: Describes the history of bridges, the various kinds,
and how they are constructed. 1. Bridges—Juvenile literature.
[1. Bridges.] I. Doty, Roy, 1922-   ill.   II. Title. TG148.C38
1992   624'.2—dc20   91-44641   CIP
ISBN: 0-671-77741-6

THE BRIDGE BOOK

by Polly Carter

illustrated by Roy Doty

SIMON & SCHUSTER BOOKS FOR YOUNG READERS

Published by Simon & Schuster
New York • London • Toronto • Sydney • Tokyo • Singapore

Why are all these bridges different?

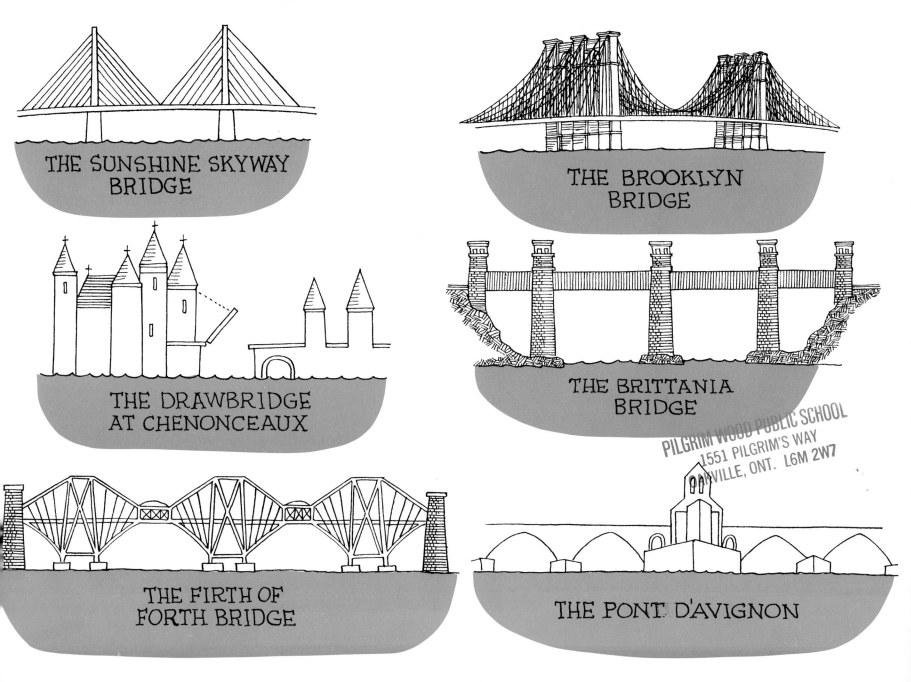

THE SUNSHINE SKYWAY
BRIDGE

THE BROOKLYN
BRIDGE

THE DRAWBRIDGE
AT CHENONCEAUX

THE BRITTANIA
BRIDGE

THE FIRTH OF
FORTH BRIDGE

THE PONT D'AVIGNON

Every bridge tells a story. Every bridge is a one-of-a-kind solution to the problem: How do I get there from here?

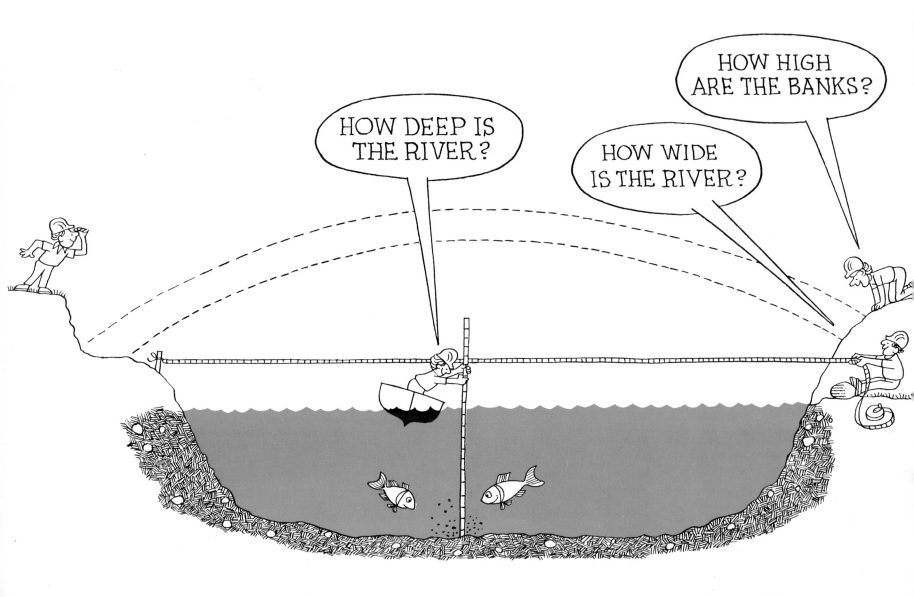

Look carefully. Every bridge is full of clues telling why and how and when it was made.

There are seven main kinds of bridges. The arch bridge, the cantilever bridge, the girder bridge, and the truss bridge are bridges that *stand* on something.

The suspension bridge and the cable-stayed bridge are bridges that *hang* from something.

The drawbridge both stands on something *and* hangs from something.

The pontoon bridge doesn't stand *or* hang. It floats on top of flat boats called pontoons.

ACTUALLY, THE FIRST PONTOON BRIDGE WE KNOW OF FLOATED ON STUFFED ANIMAL SKINS! IT WAS BUILT IN PERSIA IN 537 B.C.

In prehistoric times people struggled across a river or an abyss any way they could, without worrying about getting across the next time. Life was unpredictable, back then. There might not *be* a next time.

So the first bridges were made of logs or vines or large stones...whatever was around.

In early bridge-making days, sometimes people didn't want a bridge to be too strong. Then it could be pulled down quickly.

The Romans were the first great bridge builders. In the seventh century B.C. they built the first bridge over the Tiber River at Rome, the Pons Sublicus.

The Pons Sublicus was made of wood. It was nicknamed "The Bridge of Piles" because it sat on piles of stones. It was so narrow only three men could cross it at a time.

So when an army came to attack Rome, a Roman called Horatius offered to fight the whole army—alone. "Only three men at a time can fight me," he said. "I'll hold them off while you pull down the bridge behind me."

Two brave friends helped him fight. Horatius sent them back just before the bridge was pulled down.

When the bridge behind him collapsed, he jumped into the river and swam to safety.

The attackers were stuck on the wrong side of the Tiber.

The Pons Sublicus was convenient in wartime. But it wasn't a very strong bridge.

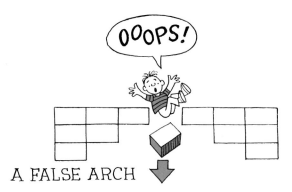

A FALSE ARCH

When bridge builders wanted bridges that would last, they molded bricks or cut stone and made an arch, or a cantilever.

THE TWO SIDES SUPPORT THE WEIGHT IN AN OVERLAPPING DIAGONAL.

The arch bridge and the cantilever bridge use the same bridge-building idea: each part depends on the part that comes before it, like steps.

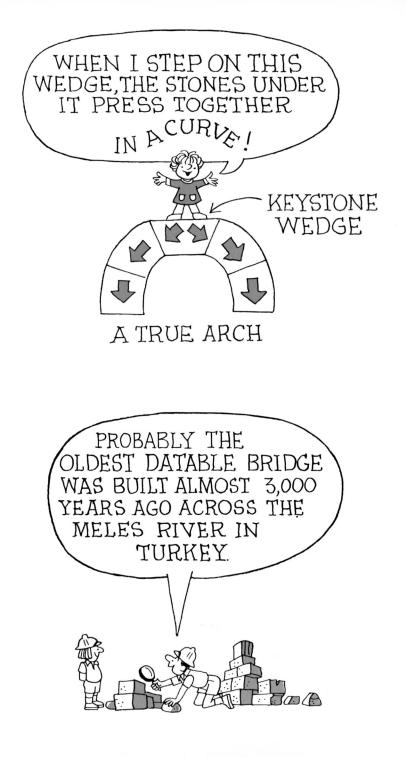

Eventually, bridge builders decided that destroying
a bridge took too much time, trouble, and money.
A better way to keep the enemy at a distance was
to build a drawbridge—which could be lifted and
lowered from only one side of a deep man-made
trench, called a moat.

But the simplest way of stopping the enemy was
to build a bridge that could double as a fort.

"PONT" IS FRENCH FOR BRIDGE.

One of the most famous fort bridges is the French arch bridge called Pont d'Avignon.

During the twelfth century, the town of Avignon expanded rapidly. Avignon badly needed a bridge, but everyone agreed it would be impossible to build one, because the Rhône river currents were so strong.

Then one day in 1177, a poor shepherd named Benoit jumped up in the middle of a church service. He said God had told him to make the bridge.

TOO MANY FLOODS!

Everyone thought the shepherd was crazy. But the bishop declared that if the boy could lift a troublesome rock no one else could move, they would all help build the bridge.

The shepherd went out to the rock. Everyone followed. The boy knelt down and prayed. Then he lifted the rock and carried it over to the river.

"It's a miracle!" said the bishop.

Benoit was canonized as St. Benezet. He started an order of monks, called the Brothers of the Bridge. After they finished the Pont d'Avignon, the monks traveled around building and fixing other bridges, to make it safer for people to travel.

Many bridges became like tiny towns, with shops and homes as well as defense towers. The Pont d'Avignon even has a chapel, supposedly made by the monks for Benezet when he died.

No one knows for sure if Benezet's story is true. But it *is* true that part of the Pont d'Avignon fell down in a flood in 1602—and that's when people started to dance on the piece of broken bridge that was left.

"CANONIZED" MEANS THE CHURCH MADE HIM A SAINT.

Floods were also a problem for American bridge builders more than two hundred years later. The little town of Coryell's Crossing, New Jersey, was the point on the Delaware River where stagecoach travelers ferried across on their way between Philadelphia and New York. At first the town was named after the Coryell family that ran the ferry, but in 1814 Captain John Lambert built a covered bridge across the river and the town's name was changed to Lambertville.

A flood in 1841 knocked the wooden bridge down, so a metal bridge was built in its place.

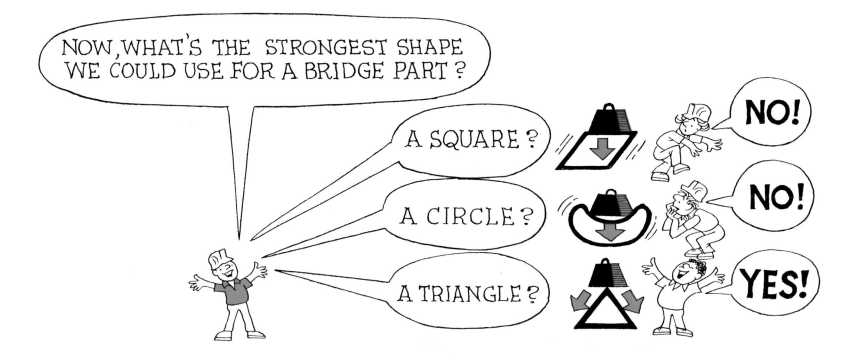

Bridges that use triangles to support the weight are called truss bridges.

The truss was invented by the great architect Andrea Palladio in Italy in the 1500s.

Truss bridges were very simple at first. But by the 1700s American bridge builders had begun to experiment. First using wood, then metal, they competed to see who could come up with the truss that was strongest, easiest, and cheapest to make. Ithiel Town, the inventor of the Town Lattice truss, even advertised that his kind of truss could be "built by the mile and cut off by the yard." Town truss bridges were so cheap and easy to make that hundreds were built in New England within just a few years.

The longest bridge in America was a trussed arch built in 1812 over the Schuylkill River at Philadelphia. In those days, a 340-foot bridge was long enough to be called the Colossus.

TOWN LATTICE
TRUSS

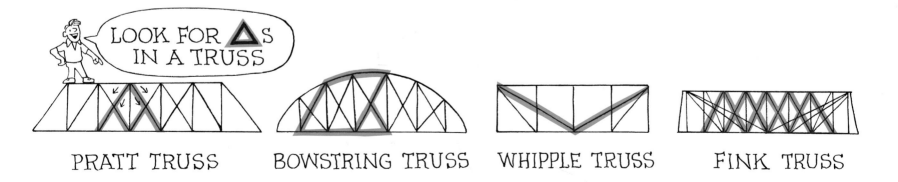

PRATT TRUSS   BOWSTRING TRUSS   WHIPPLE TRUSS   FINK TRUSS

Railroads began to crisscross America in the 1800s. Railroad bridge builders had to design bridge parts that were very simple, so they could be mass-produced. Since trains are heavy, these bridge parts also had to be extra strong.

Needing to make bridges longer and stronger, bridge builders began to invent new kinds of bridges, and started to use iron in the late 1700s, concrete in the mid-1800s, and steel in the late 1800s.

Most railroad bridges are now made of metal, since it's stronger than wood or stone.

CAST IRON IS MADE IN A MOLD. IT'S STRONG WHEN YOU PUSH ON IT BUT NOT WHEN YOU PULL.

At first, some railroad bridge builders used cast iron. But the bridges kept falling down until bridge builders started using wrought iron.

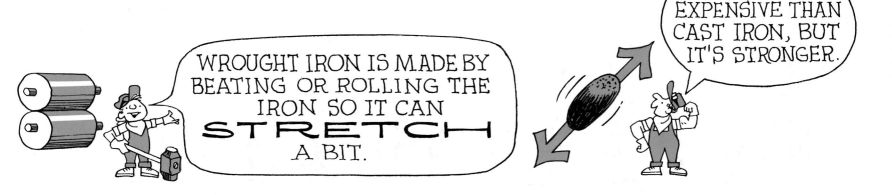

WROUGHT IRON IS MADE BY BEATING OR ROLLING THE IRON SO IT CAN STRETCH A BIT.

IT'S MORE EXPENSIVE THAN CAST IRON, BUT IT'S STRONGER.

The Firth of Tay railroad bridge in Scotland had wrought iron trusses but cast iron supports. The supports collapsed when a train crossed the Tay River during a hurricane in 1879, only two years after the bridge was built.

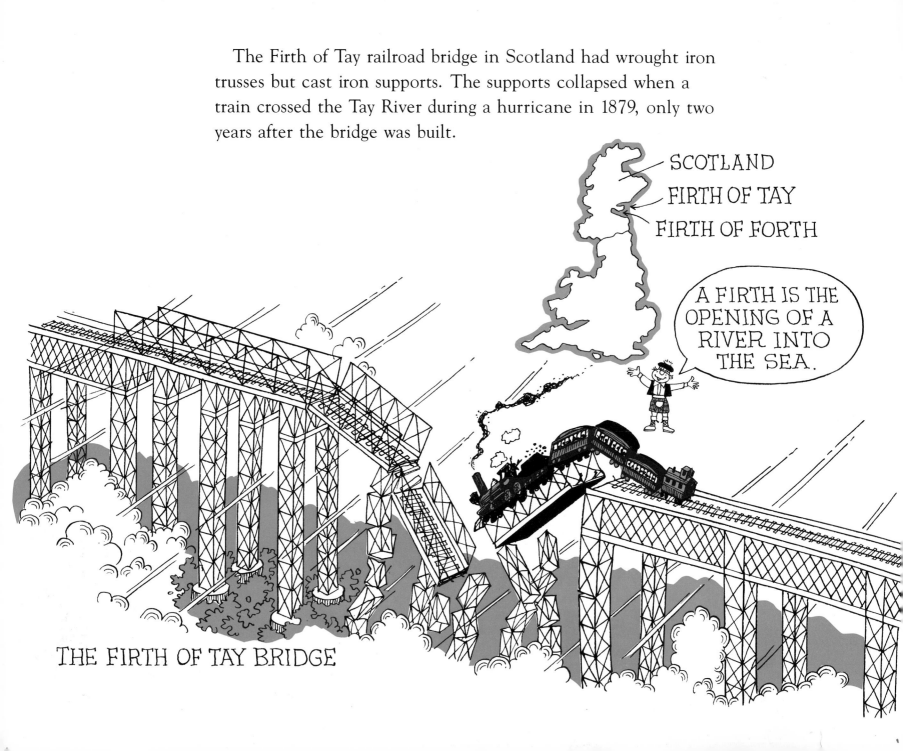

THE FIRTH OF TAY BRIDGE

So the Firth of Forth cantilever railroad bridge was built to last forever. It was *all* wrought iron.

It looks like a brontosaurus with three humps.

It was built bit by bit, starting from the rock in the middle of the firth and extending both ways to the shores. Meanwhile, the shore arms were cantilevered out to meet at the rock. The parts over water were balanced by heavy weights on both shores.

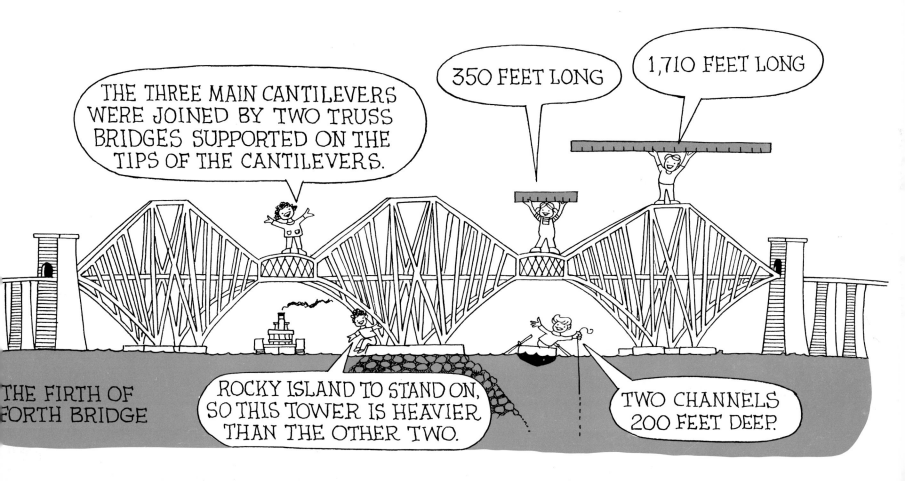

The earliest suspension bridges were prehistoric. They looked like hammocks. The problem was that they also swung like hammocks when people walked on them.

In the early 1800s, bridge builders finally figured out how to use suspension without making a swinging bridge. A suspension bridge doesn't look like a hammock anymore. Now it looks more like a sheet pinned on a clothesline.

GOLDEN GATE BRIDGE
1937
4,200 FEET

Since it only needs a pier and a tower at each end, a suspension bridge can cross a much longer distance than any other kind of bridge.

New kinds of bridges are still being invented. The cable-stayed bridge was invented in 1955. It's half suspension bridge and half cantilever bridge, because the roadway is suspended from a cable and cantilevers to both shores from one or two towers in the middle.

The Sunshine Skyway cable-stayed bridge, built in 1983 across Tampa Bay in Florida, uses the harp pattern of cables.

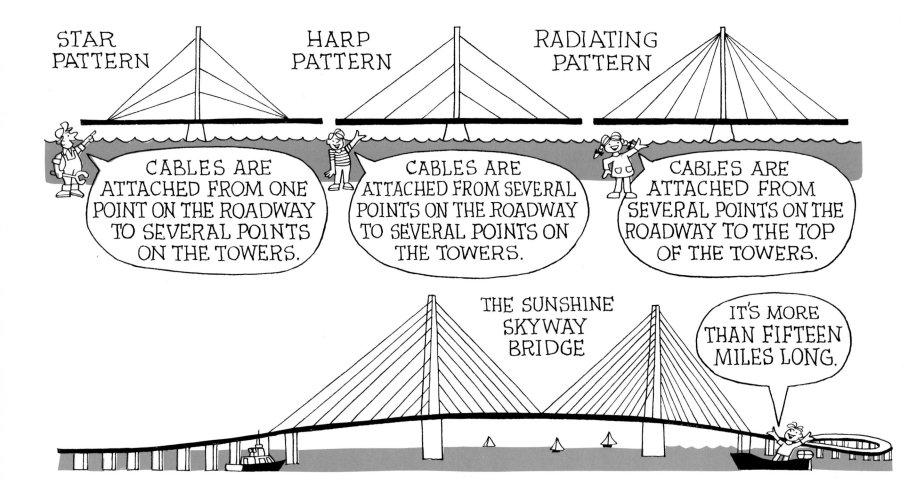

A girder bridge is simple: just beams called girders, supported by piers. Most highway bridges are girder bridges, built of concrete and factory-made steel parts.

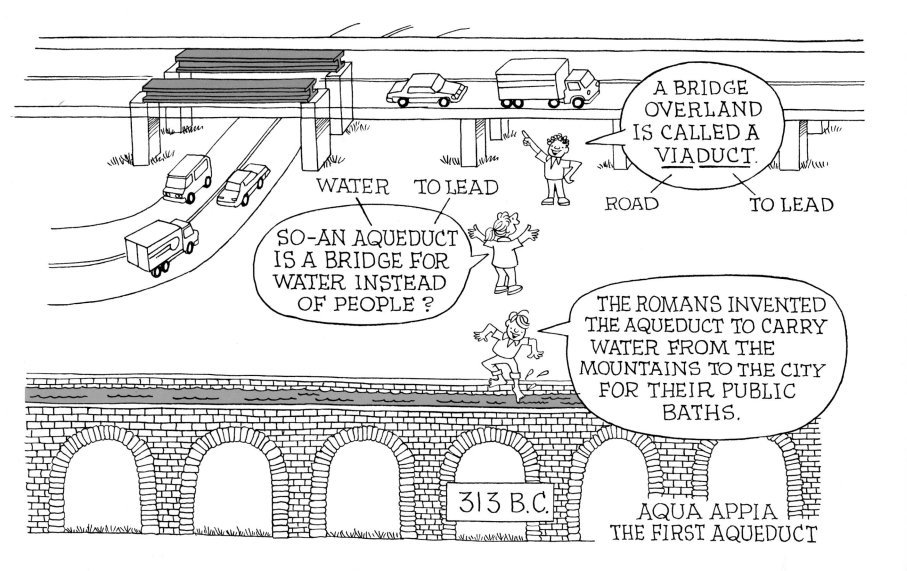

Bridge builders had to learn the hard way.
When a bridge fell down, they had to figure out why.

THE BRIDGE WASN'T THICK ENOUGH?

THE MATERIAL WASN'T STRONG ENOUGH?

The Britannia girder railroad bridge across the Menai Strait in Wales is a real solution-to-a-problem bridge.

The problem was: an iron bar that was long enough to cross the strait and strong enough to carry a train was too heavy to be moved.

A bridge builder named Robert Stephenson had a great idea.

A STRAIT IS A CHANNEL JOINING TWO BODIES OF WATER.

MENAI STRAIT

WALES

WHAT ABOUT A HOLLOW BAR? THEN TRAINS CAN GO THROUGH IT INSTEAD OF OVER IT.

Stephenson built the Britannia's hollow girders in the shape of giant rectangular tubes. Then he floated the girders into the strait and lifted them into place between the piers with huge jacks, making a 1500-foot tunnel.

It worked!

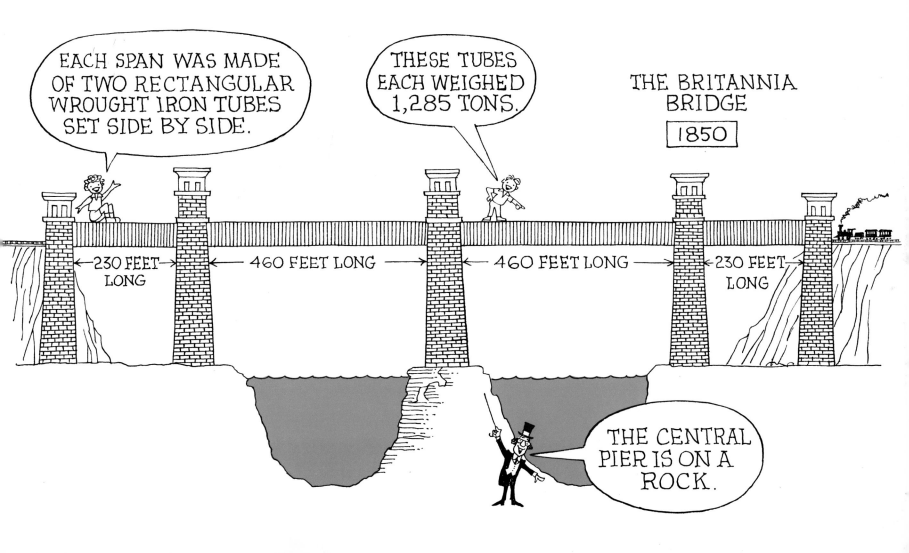

Try being a bridge detective.

The Brooklyn Bridge in New York City was begun in 1869 by a famous engineer named John Roebling. He died before the bridge was finished, so his son, Washington Roebling, took over.

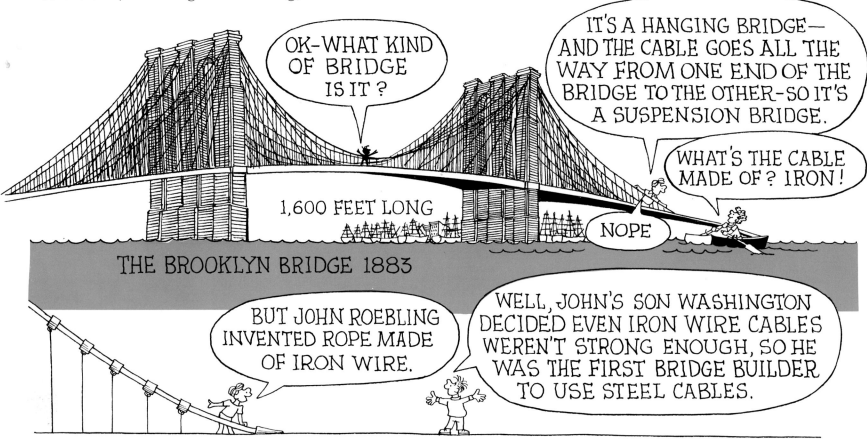

Steel can be made so hard that only a diamond can scratch it—and so flexible that it can be bent by hand without breaking. The Steel Age began in the late 1800s, when Henry Bessemer found a cheap way to produce steel from cast iron.

Did you know a heavy wind can shake a bridge down?
When the Tacoma suspension bridge in Washington State was opened in 1940, it was one of the longest bridges in the world.

But the first heavy storm made the long bridge twist in the middle. It twisted and humped up in waves until it finally broke.

Now bridge builders make sure a long bridge is extra strong, because they know anything that makes a bridge move in a wave can break it. When soldiers march in step, their feet all hit the ground at the same time. A marching army can make the earth shake. So when soldiers cross a bridge, they stop marching and walk. If they didn't break step, they might break the bridge.

No two bridges are the same.

Every bridge tells its own story: the story of the
people who built it and the people who use it.

Next time you go for a walk, a car ride, or a train
ride, be a bridge detective.

Can you name all the bridges you see?

GLOSSARY

Kinds of Bridges

▶ Aqueduct—A bridge featuring a channel to carry water. Famous example: the first aqueduct, Aqua Appia, 313 B.C. It was named after Appius Claudius Crassus, who directed its construction.

▶ Arch—A curve of stones or bricks with the topmost stone or brick cut in a wedge shape, so pressure is simultaneously directed out and down instead of simply straight down. Famous example: Pont d'Avignon, France, 1188.

▶ Cable-stayed—Girders or trusses hang by the cable from a central tower, and cantilever both ways outward from a tower. Star pattern: cables run from one point on the roadway to many points on the towers. Harp pattern: cables run from many points on the roadway to many points on the towers. Radiating pattern: cables run from many points on the roadway to the tops of the towers. Famous example: Sunshine Skyway precast-concrete bridge across Florida's Tampa Bay, 1983, 15.1 miles long: main span 1,200 feet long.

▶ Cantilever—Two beams called cantilevers extend from the two banks; two more beams—supported by the first beams—extend one from each side of the first beams; continuing on until the two extensions meet in the middle. Famous example: Firth of Forth, Scotland, 1890, 3,238 feet long; main span 1,710 feet long.

▶ Covered—A bridge roadway protected by a roof. Usually made of wood. Covered bridges were most widely used in New England during the 1700s. Example: Lambertville-Delaware, across the Delaware River from New Jersey to Pennsylvania, 1814. Destroyed in a flood, 1841.

▶ Drawbridge—A bridge hinged at one end so it can be raised and lowered. Example in a castle: Caerphilly Castle, Wales, finished in 1272. London Bridge, England, 1209, had a drawbridge to allow ships to pass—and to help control rebellions.

▶ Girder—A bridge made of beams, or girders, whose ends rest on piers or abutments. Most highway bridges are girder bridges. Famous example: the Britannia tubular iron bridge across England's Menai Strait, 1850, 1,380 feet long.

▶ Pontoon—A bridge without piers or abutments; it floats on flat-bottomed boats called pontoons. The first known pontoon bridge was built by King Cyrus of Persia in 537 B.C.; it floated on stuffed animal skins.

▶ Suspension—A roadway hanging by cables from two or more towers. Famous example: the Brooklyn Bridge, New York City, 1883, 5,989 feet long, main span 1,595 feet long; the Golden Gate Bridge, San Francisco, 1937, 8,981 feet long, main span 4,200 feet long.

▶ Truss—A roadway supported by a framework of triangles that distribute the weight outward and gradually down instead of straight down. Truss bridges abounded in America during the 1700s. Famous example: The Colossus, a trussed arch over the Schuylkill River at Philadelphia, 1812. With a 340-foot span, it was the longest wooden bridge in the country. It was destroyed in a fire in 1838.

▶ Viaduct—A bridge over land.

Parts of Bridges

▶ Abutment—The supports at each end of the bridge.

▶ Cable—Iron or steel rope from the roadway to the tower of a suspension or a cable-stayed bridge.

▶ Caisson—An underwater watertight box, open at the bottom, in which men called dredgers work, digging through sand or mud until they reach solid rock for the bridge piers to stand on.

▶ Keystone wedge—A wedge-shaped piece of stone or brick at the top curve of an arch; the more weight placed on the larger top area, the more the stones or bricks underneath it press together.

▶ Pier—The leg of a bridge; the support between the two abutments.

▶ Roadway—The part of the bridge people and vehicles travel on.

▶ Span—The distance between two adjacent bridge supports. Bridges with piers are called multi-span bridges: one pier means two spans; two piers means three spans, and so on.

▶ Tower—The part of the bridge that supports the cables of a suspension or a cable-stayed bridge.